Revised Edition

Danica Patrick

By Jeff Savage

AMAZING
ATHLETES

Lerner Publications Company • Minneapolis

Lerner Publications Company
A division of Lerner Publishing Group, Inc.
241 First Avenue North
Minneapolis, MN 55401 U.S.A.

Website address: www.lernerbooks.com

Library of Congress Cataloging-in-Publication Data

Savage, Jeff, 1961–
    Danica Patrick / by Jeff Savage. — Rev. ed.
       p. cm. — (Amazing athletes)
    Includes index.
    ISBN 978-0-7613-5750-6 (lib. bdg. : alk. paper)
    1. Patrick, Danica, 1982–—Juvenile literature. 2. Automobile racing drivers—United States—
Biography—Juvenile literature. 3. Women automobile racing drivers—United States—Biography—
Juvenile literature. I. Title.
    GV1032.P38S38 2011
    796.72092—dc22 [B]   2009035644

Manufactured in the United States of America
1 — BP — 7/15/10

TABLE OF CONTENTS

Danica races down the track in Motegi, Japan.

FIRST LADY

Danica Patrick roared down the racetrack at more than 200 miles per hour. Her car was getting low on fuel. But this was no time to make a **pit stop**. Danica was racing in the 2008 Japan 300 in Motegi, Japan. She was in fourth place with only a few **laps** to go.

Danica was trying to make history. No woman had ever won an **Indy Racing League** (IRL) event before. Danica had finished fourth at the Japan 300 in 2005. But she was aiming for a better finish in 2008.

With only four laps to go, Danica trailed **veteran** drivers Dan Wheldon, Tony Kanaan, and Helio Castroneves. When Wheldon and Kanaan were forced to pit stop, Danica jumped into second place. Her heart thudded against her ribs. First place was in sight! Would Danica be able to overtake Castroneves?

Danica, in the second race car, waits to make her move.

Danica *(front)* stays focused as she waits for her chance to take the lead.

Race cars must stop in the pits during races to fill their fuel tanks. Castroneves was running out of fuel. He knew that if he made a pit stop, Danica would pass him. Instead of stopping, Castroneves slowed down to save fuel. This was the chance Danica had been waiting for.

On her radio, Danica's **crew engineer**, Kyle Moyer, told Danica that she had enough fuel to finish the race. That's what she wanted to hear. With about three laps to go, it was now or never. Danica told herself, "Hey, kick it up a notch and get by. If this is what it comes down to, you better not think to yourself I wish I had tried a little bit harder."

Danica makes her move with just a few laps to go.

Danica passed Castroneves on lap 198 of the 200-lap race. She crossed the finish line fewer than six seconds ahead of Castroneves for the victory. Danica became the first woman to win an IRL event!

Danica nears the finish line as the checkered flag is waved.

N RING MOTEGI

Danica celebrated in **Victory Lane** with her family and **crew** after the race. She was happy to have finally won her first event. "I've been asked so many times when and if I can win my first race," she said. "And, finally, no more of those questions."

For one day in Japan, Danica was on top of the racing world. "That [victory] was a big relief. A long time I've waited for this," she said. But there would be many challenges ahead for Danica, including a move to a whole new kind of racing.

Danica poses with her trophy after winning the Japan 300.

Karting is a popular sport around the world. Danica raced against other kids her age in karts like these.

CATCHING ON

Danica Sue Patrick was born March 25, 1982, in Beloit, Wisconsin. She grew up in the town of Roscoe in northern Illinois. Her father, T.J., was a champion snowmobile racer. Her mother, Bev, was a car mechanic. The two had met at a snowmobile race.

Danica was not interested in cars as a young girl. She preferred playing with Barbie dolls. "She was a girlie girl," said her mother. "She didn't want to get grease under her fingernails."

When Danica was 10, her younger sister Brooke asked to try driving a go-kart. Danica decided to go too. In her first attempt at driving, Danica swerved to miss a truck in the parking lot and crashed head-on into a concrete wall. Fortunately, she was wearing her seat belt and helmet. She was not hurt.

Soon Danica got the hang of driving the karts. "I loved the way you could see yourself get better in racing," said Danica. "I'd go around the track in maybe 52 seconds. I'd come in and ask my dad. 'Was that 51?' Then I'd say, 'OK, let's do 50. Let's do 49, 48. Seeing the improvement was so satisfying."

A few months later, Brooke crashed four times in one race. She gave up go-karting. But Danica was hooked. Before long, she had broken the track record at Sugar River Raceway in southern Wisconsin.

In 1993, Danica began competing in **World Karting Association** (WKA) events. She finished fourth in one series of races and second in another. Some boys and their parents were jealous. Danica understood. "No dad wants his boy beaten by a little girl," she said. But plenty of boys lost to Danica. A year later, she

Like Danica, many of the world's great race car drivers grew up racing go-karts. They include four-time NASCAR champion Jeff Gordon, two-time NASCAR champion Tony Stewart, and seven-time Formula One world champion Michael Schumacher.

About 100,000 Americans enjoy the sport of karting on racetracks. Go-karts are about 6 feet long and 4 feet wide. They weigh about 150 pounds. Kids can begin racing karts at the age of five.

won her first national points championship. She won more titles in 1995 and 1996.

Danica was also active at Hononegah High School. She was a cheerleader and played volleyball and basketball. She sang in the school choir and played flute in the band. But her true passion was racing. In 1996, she competed in 49 races. She won 39 of them! "But it was never good enough," she told herself. "I could always be better."

Danica in front of her Formula Vauxhall car in Great Britain in 1998.

GOING PLACES

Danica dared to be great. At the age of 14, she took a course taught by former Indy 500 driver Lyn St. James. She learned to eat healthy foods and how to concentrate while racing. St. James was impressed with her young student. "She was talented, committed, and poised," said St. James.

When Danica turned 16, she was invited to race in the Formula Vauxhall Series in Europe. She would race against other young drivers in small, lightweight race cars. With her parents' permission, she quit school during her junior year in high school. She moved alone to Milton Keynes, England.

"England is a great place for racing. It was my college," said Danica. Her only regret was not graduating from high school with her classmates. But she did get her **general equivalency diploma (GED)**. In Great Britain, Danica stayed with her friends and slept on the living room couch for two months. Then she moved into a tiny bedroom the size of a closet.

Danica races in a Formula Vauxhall Series event in 1998 while in Great Britain.

Danica lived and breathed racing. Her hard work paid off. In just her first full year, she finished an amazing ninth in the Vauxhall **points standings**. But some of the male drivers did not welcome her. They didn't like competing against a girl.

Danica knows it is important to always work hard. "You can go from zero to hero and back again really fast," she says. "You have to keep moving. You have to keep thinking, 'I can be better.' You have to be persistent."

And they really didn't like finishing races behind a girl. "It was boys being boys," said Danica. "I got really cold and just hard. I had to be. I had to get tough. It forced me to grow up very quickly."

Danica missed her family. She returned home to Roscoe from time to time. She enjoyed working at the family-owned Java Hut coffee shop.

But after being away from the track for a few weeks, Danica would hurry back to Great Britain for more racing.

As Danica improved, she moved up into faster and tougher racing leagues. She dreamed of becoming a driver in a big-time league like the IRL or **Championship Auto Racing Teams (CART)**. But would a top-level racing team trust a woman to drive their race car?

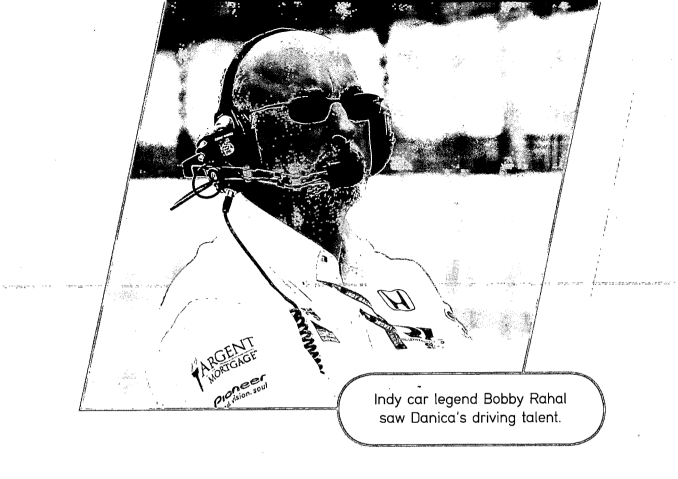

Indy car legend Bobby Rahal saw Danica's driving talent.

INTO THE BIG TIME

In 2000, Danica's performance caught the attention of Bobby Rahal. Rahal was a former CART champion and Indy 500 winner. He and late-night TV star David Letterman owned the Rahal Letterman Racing team.

Danica pushes her car to the limit during a Barber Dodge Pro Series race in 2002.

"There are lots of talented drivers," Rahal said. "But few make the sacrifices that Danica has. She is serious enough to do whatever it takes." In 2002, Rahal offered Danica a three-year **contract** to drive a car for his team. Danica eagerly accepted.

Rahal told Danica that if she worked hard, she would get a chance to race in the IRL. But first, Danica raced in the 2002 **Barber Dodge Pro Series**. This was a circuit where young drivers developed their skills. In her first race in Toronto, she finished a very good seventh.

Three weeks later in Vancouver, she did even better, finishing fourth.

In 2003, Danica moved up to the next level, the **Toyota Atlantic Series**. At the Monterrey Grand Prix in Mexico, she finished third and became the first woman to earn a place on the **podium**. In the season finale in Miami, she finished a season-best second. For the year, she ranked sixth in overall points.

Josh Hunt's car crashes over Danica's car during a 2004 Toyota Atlantic Series race.

Danica was working harder than ever. She ran nearly five miles each day. She strengthened her body with weight training. She ate only healthy foods, especially fish, fruits, and vegetables. She drank plenty of her favorite beverage—water. In 2004, she finished in the top five in 10 of the 12 races she entered. She was the only driver to complete every lap of every race. She was ready to compete against some of the world's best drivers in the IRL.

Danica became very popular. Young girls gave her handmade bracelets. Male college students lined up to pose for pictures with her.

Danica looks serious as she prepares for the 2005 Indianapolis 500.

A NEW CHALLENGE

The night before Danica drove her first Indy car, she barely slept. "I woke up about every 20 minutes," she said. But when Danica actually drove the powerful car, she soon saw that she could control it. In her fourth IRL race at the 2005 Japan 300, she finished an impressive fourth.

Danica *(top)* is confident on the racetrack. But she doesn't take unnecessary chances.

Then came the Indianapolis 500. Nearly three hours into the race, with 10 laps left, Danica found herself in the lead! Unfortunately, she was almost out of gas. She had to slow down. Danica crossed the finish line in fourth place. "I got to lead my first Indy 500. I actually had a chance to win the race," she said. "I accomplished a lot."

Danica raced well her **rookie** year but did not get a win. "As long as we keep working hard, the wins will come," she said. Danica did work hard, and her first win came at the 2008 Japan 300.

Danica's performances made headlines in newspapers across the country. Her picture appeared on the cover of *Sports Illustrated* magazine. It was the first time an IRL driver had been on the cover in 20 years. "DanicaMania" swept the country. Sales of Danica hats, key chains, and other products went through the roof. Reporters swarmed Danica.

Danica is the center of attention before and after every race.

With her popularity at an all-time high, Danica decided to try something new. She agreed to participate in a few 2010 races run by the **National Association for Stock Car Auto Racing (NASCAR)**. Stock cars look like the cars that people see on the road every day. But they have much bigger engines. NASCAR is the most popular car racing league in the United States. Would Danica fit in with some of the world's best stock car drivers?

Danica on the red carpet at the 2009 ESPY Awards. She is one of racing's most well-known drivers.

Danica poses with her new stock car *(left)* and her Indy car in December 2009.

Driving a stock car would be a big challenge for Danica. She would face all new racetracks and drivers. She would also have to learn to handle her new car. But Danica knows how to deal with new challenges. "You've got to take things in small steps. Baby steps," she said. "Let's see if I like [NASCAR]." Danica raced in her first NASCAR event in February 2010 at Daytona International Speedway.

Danica is so popular with racing fans that companies have asked her to **sponsor** their products. She earns millions of dollars to **endorse** cars, clothes, and websites.

As Danica keeps proving herself on the racetrack, people might stop thinking of her as a woman in a man's sport. But Danica already knows that she fits in with the best drivers in the world. "I've always raced against the guys and I just see myself as one of them," she says. "I'm just a racer who happens to be a woman."

Danica poses in an ad that encourages people to drink milk.

Selected Career Highlights

2010 Finished sixth in her first NASCAR race at Daytona International Speedway

2009 Finished third at the Indianapolis 500

2008 Finished first at the Japan 300 in Montegi, Japan

2007 Finished eighth at the Indianapolis 500

2006 Finished eighth at the Indianapolis 500

2005 Finished fourth at the Indianapolis 500
Named IRL Rookie of the Year

2004 Finished third in the Toyota Atlantic Series championship with 269 points
Had 10 top-five finishes in 12 races
Only driver in the Atlantic 12-race series to complete every lap
Became first female driver to win pole position in the Toyota Atlantic Series at Round 5 at Portland, Oregon

2003 Finished sixth in the Toyota Atlantic Series Championship with 269 points
Had 5 top-five finishes in 12 races
Became first female to post a podium (top three) result in the 30-year history of the Toyota Atlantic Series at Monterrey, Mexico

2002 Captured the pole and won the Toyota Pro/Celebrity Race at the Long Beach Grand Prix
Finished fourth at Vancouver for her highest finish

2001 Won the Gorsline Scholarship award for the top upcoming road racing driver

2000 Finished second at the Formula Ford Festival in Great Britain, the highest-ever finish for an American in 26 years

1999 Finished ninth in the Formula Vauxhall Championship in Great Britain

1998 Made debut in Great Britain at the age of 16 in the Formula Vauxhall Series

1997 Won the World Karting Association (WKA) Grand National Championship HPV class

1996 Won 39 of 49 karting races

Glossary

Barber Dodge Pro Series: formerly CART's third circuit. In this league, drivers competed in identical cars. Pro Series racers hoped to move up to CART's next level, the Toyota Atlantic Series.

Championship Auto Racing Teams (CART): formerly the top American open-wheel racing league. CART became the Champ Car World Series in 2004.

contract: a written agreement

crew: the members of a racing team who build and repair the cars

crew engineer: the main crew member in charge of the engine of the car

endorse: to show support or approval of a product in exchange for money

general equivalency diploma (GED): a certificate that can serve as a high school diploma

go-kart: a small, flat, one-person vehicle with a motor

Indy Racing League: one of the top (with the Champ Car World Series) U.S. open-wheel racing leagues. Indy cars race on oval and road tracks across the United States.

junior year: third of four years in high school or college

lap: a complete trip around a racetrack

National Association for Stock Car Auto Racing (NASCAR): founded in 1947, NASCAR is the governing body of stock car racing. It says which changes to a car's engine and body are allowed to make it a stock car.

pit stop: a stop during a race in an area where a car can be fixed or gassed up

podium: the platform on which the top-three finishers in a race stand to receive their awards

points standings: a list that shows how many points each driver has earned. Points are awarded based on place of finish. The driver with the most points is at the top of the list.

rookie: a first-year player or driver in a sport or league

sponsor: to give financial support

Toyota Atlantic Series: formerly CART's second circuit. Toyota Atlantic Series drivers hope to earn a spot in one of the sport's top circuits, such as the Indy Racing League.

veteran: a racer who has competed for several years

Victory Lane: a road extending from the racetrack that the winning car drives along when celebrating a win

World Karting Association: the main organization that oversees go-kart races

Further Reading & Websites

Doeden, Matt. *Stock Cars.* Minneapolis: Lerner Publications Company, 2007.

Fish, Bruce. *Indy-Car Racing.* Philadelphia: Chelsea House Publishers, 2006.

Piehl, Janet. *Indy Race Cars.* Minneapolis: Lerner Publications Company, 2007.

Stewart, Mark, and Mike Kennedy. *NASCAR in the Driver's Seat.* Minneapolis: Lerner Publications Company, 2008.

Danica's Website
http://www.danicaracing.com
Danica's official website features trivia, photos, records, and information about Danica, her race car, and the IRL.

Indy Racing League
http://www.indyracing.com
The IRL's website provides fans with recent news stories, statistics, schedules, and biographies of drivers and teams.

NASCAR.com
http://www.nascar.com
NASCAR's official website has the latest standings, news stories, videos, and much more for fans of all ages.

Sports Illustrated Kids
http://www.sikids.com
The *Sports Illustrated Kids* website covers all sports, including auto racing.

World Karting Association
http://www.worldkarting.com
Learn more about the fun and exciting sport of go-kart racing from the official site of the World Karting Association.

Index

Photo Acknowledgments

The images in this book are used with the permission of: © AFP/AFP/ Getty Images, pp. 4, 6; AP Photo/Shuji Kajiyama, p. 5; AP Photo/Katsumi Kasahara, pp. 7, 8; Kyodo via AP Images, p. 9; © Alexander Hubrich/CORBIS, p. 10; Sutton-Images.com, pp. 14, 16, 21; © AJ Mast/Icon SMI, p. 19; © Darrell Ingham/Getty Images, p. 20; © Robert Mora/Getty Images, p. 22; © Jeff Roberts/AFP/Getty Images, p. 23; © Gavin Lawrence/Getty Images, pp. 24, 25; © Kevin Mazur/WireImage/Getty Images, p. 26; © Joshua Lott/Getty Images, p. 27; © Jonathan Ferrey/Getty Images, p. 28; AP Photo/Butch Dill, p. 29.

Front Cover: AP Photo/John Bazemore.